Day Hikes and Short Walks

of Grand Teton National Park

Written by
Charles Craighead

Photography by
Henry H. Holdsworth

**Official Guidebook
of Grand Teton National Park**

Published by
Grand Teton Natural History Association

Table *of* Contents

Hiking the Tetons and the Park

When the first superintendent of Grand Teton National Park, Samuel Woodring, arrived in 1929, he set out to build a system of trails he envisioned as one of the best in the country. Working with a limited Depression Era budget, and inspiring a lot of hard work, he had his crews start mapping and cutting trails. By 1935 there were over 90 miles of developed trails, with much of the hardest labor being provided by the Civilian Conservation Corps. The CCC was one of President Franklin Roosevelt's programs providing jobs for young men on public lands. Among other tasks, they cut trails through the rock, built bridges, and developed campgrounds.

Today over 250 miles of trails criss-cross the park. Some are traveled almost daily, while others see only an occasional hiker. Trails range from perfectly level paths through the park's meadows to steep scrambles up and over rock outcroppings. Overall, the trails in the Tetons are well-made, well-maintained, and a joy to walk.

The steep rise of the Tetons can intimidate visitors, but in fact they are one of the most accessible mountain ranges. Within just a mile or two of some of the trailheads, hikers can experience the mountain canyons or enjoy the view from high up on the slopes. Wildlife and wildflowers are found in all parts of the park, so you don't have to go far to have the chance of seeing something.

The hikes in this book are intended to introduce visitors to the variety and beauty of the park trail system. These are the hikes that can be done in an easy day, or less, by most hikers. More experienced hikers might consider some of these as strolls, but most of the hikes can be expanded and lengthened for a more rigorous outing. For visitors who want to visit the backcountry or plot out a longer route, more detailed hiking and trail guides are available at the park's visitor centers.

Most of all, these trails provide an opportunity to appreciate the natural history, geology, and human history of the park. Although we've given destinations and

Mount Moran at sunrise from Oxbow Bend

landmarks, there's a lot to be said for just strolling down the trail at a leisurely pace and enjoying what's along the path. After all, it was the simple beauty of the valley and its picture-perfect mountains that inspired people like John D. Rockefeller to preserve it all for later generations.

The trails in Grand Teton National Park fall into three broad groups: 1) the trail system exploring the lakes, moraines, and forests of the valley floor; 2) the trail system leading into the mountains via the canyons and ridges; and 3) the backcountry network of trails. This guide focuses mainly on the valley trails and a few of the trails that go into the canyons and lower mountain areas. These are all established, well-marked and well-maintained paths.

These trails can be hiked wearing comfortable walking or running shoes, or light hiking boots. Visitors should prepare for a full day regardless of the destination, since the duration of the outing can lengthen from the effects of high altitude on energy levels, changing weather, or just finding interesting things to stop for along the trail. This usually means bringing along some water and food, a raincoat, a hat and gloves, and a sweater or light jacket. The mountain weather can change dramatically in a few hours and temperatures can drop considerably.

A few biting insects appear at times, especially near the lakes and streams. Insect repellent can help make the day more enjoyable. The air at this altitude is thin and blocks little of the sun's ultraviolet rays, so sunburn protection should be worn.

Black bears inhabit most of the canyons and the forests at the base of the mountains, but for the most part they are shy and nonaggressive. However, you should always give them a wide berth and make noise to alert them to your presence. Be especially alert for nearby cubs and don't get between them and the mother. Park rangers can give you detailed information on hiking in bear country. All large animals, such as moose and elk, should be left alone and not approached.

View south from Granite Canyon Trailhead

From the Granite Canyon Trailhead and Teton Village

Other than a few half-hearted attempts at ranching by homesteaders in the early 1900s, Granite Canyon was left alone for many years. With the development of the Jackson Hole ski area and its aerial tram to the top of Rendezvous Peak just outside the park at Teton Village, the canyon became a popular hiking area.

Granite Canyon is the park's southernmost canyon, offering the first access point to the backcountry from that direction. In this area of the mountains the geology changes to softer rock than the main Teton peaks to the north, and the peaks aren't as high or abrupt. Beautiful scenery and quieter and less visited trails than the central parts of the Tetons make this canyon special.

Granite Canyon Trailhead sits right on the Moose–Wilson Road, just north of the park's southern entrance station. Horseback parties use it as a departure point for the backcountry, and hikes originating at the top of the nearby aerial ski tram end here. Located in the center of Teton Village, out through the park entrance and a few miles south of the Granite Canyon Trailhead, the aerial tram provides effortless access to the high country within the park for a fee.

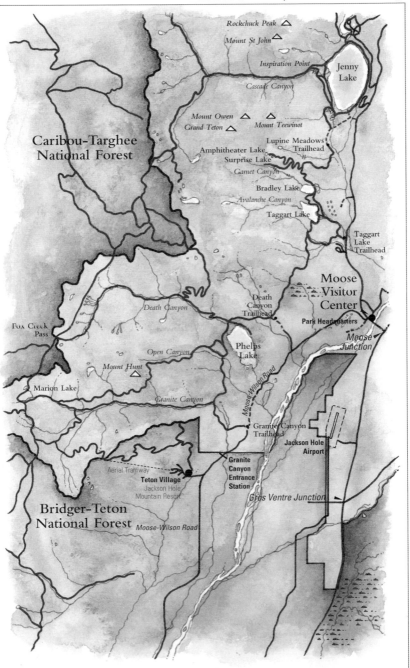

Rockchuck Peak △

Mount St John △

Inspiration Point

Jenny Lake

Cascade Canyon

Mount Owen △   △

Grand Teton △   Mount Teewinot

Lupine Meadows
Trailhead

Amphitheater Lake

Surprise Lake

Garnet Canyon

**Caribou-Targhee
National Forest**

Bradley Lake

Avalanche Canyon

Taggart Lake

Taggart
Lake
Trailhead

**Moose
Visitor
Center**

Death
Canyon
Trailhead

Park Headquarters

Death Canyon

Fox Creek
Pass

Phelps
Lake

**Moose
Junction**

Open Canyon

Mount Hunt △

Marion Lake

Granite Canyon

Granite Canyon
Trailhead

Moose-Wilson Road

**Jackson Hole
Airport**

Aerial Tramway

Teton Village
*Jackson Hole
Mountain Resort*

**Granite
Canyon
Entrance
Station**

Gros Ventre Junction

**Bridger-Teton
National Forest**   *Moose-Wilson Road*

To the Death Canyon Trailhead

6.6 miles, one way

This is a moderately easy hike, but probably makes a full day with all the stops and ups-and-downs along the way. It starts at the Granite Canyon Trailhead and climbs slowly for about 1.5 miles, up onto the moraine. There's an intersection here with the Valley Trail, and you go right toward Phelps Lake.

The trail pretty much follows the base of the mountains through mixed forest and meadows. It climbs up a few hundred feet along the way, crosses streams, and eventually drops back down toward Phelps Lake. Here it passes several intersections with trails coming in from the left, but it continues on around to the end of the lake and then climbs steeply up some switchbacks to the Phelps Lake Overlook. From here it's an easy mile downhill to the Death Canyon Trailhead.

Solitude, wildflowers, and some good exercise make this a good overall hike. While it isn't as spectacular as hikes in the main Teton peak area, it's fairly wild and little-traveled. Most of the visitor use will be from the trailhead to the first junction and then from Phelps Lake to the Death Canyon Trailhead. The 3.5 mile stretch in between should be quiet. Birds, elk, deer, and an occasional black bear inhabit the area.

Granite Canyon

As far as you want, up to 12.8 miles round trip to the upper Patrol Cabin

Lower Granite Canyon

Granite Canyon offers quick access into the mountains. For many years it was used almost exclusively by horse-back parties from nearby dude ranches. After an easy 1.5 mile walk from the trailhead to the Valley Trail junction, turn right for a little ways to the left intersection with the Granite Canyon Trail. From this point you can walk as far as you like up the canyon.

The relatively lush lower Granite Canyon usually has a lot of wildflowers early in the season. It's also a great place for bird-watching in the various kinds of habitat the trail passes through. There are boulder fields, stands of Douglas Fir, and all kinds of flowering shrubs and berries in between.

The trail passes a patrol cabin and heads up along the north side of the canyon. It enters a long camping zone area and eventually, after almost 5 miles, reaches a second patrol cabin. This marks the farthest turnaround point for a day hike, although fit hikers with an early start often continue on to Marion Lake, another 3.5 miles.

From the Jackson Hole Mountain Resort Aerial Tram to the Granite Canyon Trailhead

11.6 miles, almost all downhill (4,100 feet elevation drop)

Jackson Hole Mountain Resort aerial tram

This hike wasn't possible until Teton Village and the ski area opened in 1966, and the aerial tram began operation. Now you can make a full day hike and go downhill (mostly) all the way. Even with the tram doing the initial work, this is considered a difficult hike.

The hike begins at the top of the tram, but seasonal snow conditions may limit use of the upper trails in the spring and early summer. Tram operators will have up-to-date information on trail conditions.

From the top of Rendezvous Peak, follow the trail to the first intersection and turn right toward the Granite Canyon Trail. This area is all above the timber line, and it's the easiest way to experience alpine conditions. The trail descends into a deep cirque, climbs up the other side, and then descends again into a forested area with camping sites. Along the way, especially in midsummer, there are often incredible shows of alpine wildflowers.

At 3.5 miles from the top of the tram, there's a trail intersection and a right turn to Granite Canyon. This path goes down just over 1.5 miles to the Upper Granite Patrol Cabin, where it turns right and goes all the way down to the Granite Canyon Trailhead, a little over 6 miles away.

This is a fairly long hike, almost 12 miles, and it can be hard on the knees and other joints going downhill. But the opportunity to get out into the alpine scenery without having to climb up to it is worth the effort.

Short Strolls

Mule deer

From the trailhead it's an easy walk toward the first trail intersection as far as you want to go. It can be hot during midday, but in early and late hours there may be deer or elk out in the open. The aerial tram offers a stroll around the top of the mountain for panoramic scenery and alpine wildflowers.

Trail to Death Canyon

From the Death Canyon Trailhead

Located in a thick Lodgepole Pine forest, the Death Canyon Trailhead accesses a large glacial moraine that curves away from the mouth of the canyon, forming Phelps Lake. This lateral moraine was created along the side of the last glacier that helped carve the canyon.

One of the major canyons of the park, Death Canyon has inherent beauty and accessibility that made it desirable to early valley residents. A 1908 dude ranch at the south end of Phelps Lake, the JY Ranch, was later owned by the Rockefeller family until they donated it to the park. The JY and the White Grass Ranch, not far from the trailhead, were two of the oldest dude ranches in the valley.

Death Canyon saw other activity early in the twentieth century when prospectors and miners tried to find gold in the upper parts of the canyon. It was also used on some occasions for travel into and out of the valley from Idaho. The Death Canyon Trail was constructed in 1920-21, and was connected in the backcountry to Cascade Canyon in 1933.

Approaching Death Canyon (left)   *Taggart Lake (overleaf)*

11

Phelps Lake

To Phelps Lake/Death Canyon

1.8 miles round trip to the Phelps Lake Overlook, 3.2 round trip to the Death Canyon Trail junction, 4 miles round trip to lake shore, 7.2 miles round trip to the Death Canyon patrol cabin

The Death Canyon Trailhead waits at the end of a rocky, winding road, with several parking spots opening up as you get close to the end. This trailhead essentially sits on the Valley Trail, a major north–south route that follows the base of the mountains from Teton Village to Lupine Meadows. Just a short ways from the trailhead you join that trail and go left toward Death Canyon.

It's just under a mile to the Phelps Lake Overlook, most of it uphill but gradual and scenic. This first mile contains one of the great wildflower shows in the park, and deer are common. The trail goes through several habitat changes to reach the overlook. The walk is rewarding just for the view, especially for photographers who arrive early in the morning.

The trail then descends about 600 feet in a series of long switchbacks to the lake level. The trail forks here, going to the left towards Open Canyon, and also to a side trail to the campground on the nearby lakeshore. This is a nice area to spend the day if you don't want to hike further.

If you turn right at the Death Canyon junction, you'll start up into the canyon. The trail drops down into a dense and beautiful forest for a bit before beginning to climb steadily upward. This eventually turns into one of the steepest trails in the park, but you can turn around anywhere. It's reasonably easy to hike a mile or so until you can see the broad expanse of the canyon ahead.

To the Taggart Lake Parking Area

5.3 miles via Taggart Lake

The Valley Trail links to this trailhead, making it a good spot to get dropped off for a hike to another trailhead. One interesting path, going right when you hit the Valley Trail junction, will take you to Taggart Lake after about four miles.

The trail follows the base of the Tetons in a relatively flat path, going through mixed forest, meadows, across small creeks, and visiting all kinds of bird and wildlife habitat.

This is prime elk country, and in the early or late hours they'll be out in the meadows. The forested trail often produces sightings of woodland birds including Goshawk, Cooper's Hawk, Gray Jay, or an occasional Great Gray Owl.

This trail remains little-used and generally offers peace and quiet. Once you reach the Taggart Lake portion of the trail there will be other hikers, but if you take the Beaver Creek fork to the right just before you reach Taggart Lake you'll avoid most people.

You'll also get a good perspective on the effects of the wildfire that burned all around Taggart Lake. It started in the forest near the trail, and winds carried it north over the moraine and around the lake.

Short Strolls

From any of the parking spots you can walk back down the unpaved road and look at the remains of the old White Grass Ranch. Or, you can walk up the trail and look at wildflowers. There are a number of small streams that the trail crosses soon after leaving the trailhead, and they support all kinds of flowers.

From the Lupine Meadows Trailhead

Many of the destinations reached from this trailhead require an early start, so it can be busy first thing in the morning as hikers and climbers start off. Mountain climbers use this trail to get to the Grand Teton and other nearby peaks. Lupine Meadows nestles right at the foot of the mountains, and it's a beautiful place in itself. Hikers who get a sunrise start are commonly greeted by elk or deer in the meadows.

Many of the cabins sitting on the east end of the meadow, close to Cottonwood Creek, are left from homesteaded property of the early 1900s. For many years guest cabins, a store, a gas station, and other commercial enterprises existed in Lupine Meadows. All private property was eventually sold to the National Park Service, and most of the old buildings were torn down. The few remaining cabins now house seasonal park employees.

Lupine Meadows remains the center of the park's mountain rescue operations. The Jenny Lake Rangers launch their search and rescue efforts from cabins and a helicopter landing site near Cottonwood Creek.

Surprise Lake and Amphitheater Lake

9.6 miles round trip 3,000 ft elevation gain

Surprise and Amphitheater Lakes sit in a small basin area scoured out of the mountainside by glaciers, nearly 3,000 feet above the valley floor. Despite the elevation gain and the distance, many visitors make this hike. It is the only trail that leads directly up the face of the mountains. Spectacular views of the peaks unfold above and the entire valley spreads out below. Even on a day of low clouds, the picturesque lakes are worth the hike.

From the Lupine Meadows Trailhead, follow the path up to the junction with the Bradley Lake Trail. Here the Surprise Lake Trail begins to switch-back across the face of the mountain, gaining elevation at each turn. At 3 miles from the trailhead there's another junction, with the Garnet Canyon Trail to the left. Most mountain climbers will turn left here to reach the Grand Teton.

Go right, and it's another steep 1.5 miles of switchbacks to Surprise Lake. The Surprise Lake area was popular as far back as the 1920s, when horse-back parties came here to camp on their way to visit the Teton Glacier, just to the north.

These lakes straddle the border between the subalpine and alpine environments and offer a great place to observe the effects of altitude on trees, search for alpine flowers, and get a close view of the peaks. Majestic Whitebark Pines grow all around the lakes.

Surprise Lake (right)

Garnet Canyon as viewed from the valley

Garnet Canyon

8.2 miles round trip, 2,100 ft elevation gain

From Lupine Meadows, the first 3 miles of this trail follow the same route as the hike to Surprise Lake to the point where the trail sign marks the fork to the left, toward Garnet Canyon. The trail then traverses the side of the mountain and turns west into Garnet. Spectacular views, both down the steep slopes into the bottom of Garnet Canyon and up the canyon to the surrounding mountains, make this an impressive walk.

The trail hugs the north side of Garnet Canyon and climbs through rocky terrain, finally reaching the creek, where it ends. From this point on, mountaineering and off-trail skills are needed. This canyon has a much different, more mountainous feel than the broader Cascade or Paintbrush Canyons.

In early summer, when its south-facing slopes first warm up, this trail abounds with wildflowers. Deer or moose feed on the lower slopes, and black bears are not uncommon. This habitat also supports lots of mountain birds such as nutcrackers, grosbeaks, and ravens.

Short Strolls

The Lupine Meadows Trailhead usually fills all of its parking spaces early, but late in the day it's a nice place to park and walk. Stroll down the level trail as it follows the base of the mountains, and when it turns uphill go as far as you like. There are dozens of wildflowers, good chances for elk or deer sightings, and lots of birds. Ospreys sometimes nest on top of one of the pine trees along here.

Lupine Meadows and Mount Teewinot (right)

Taggart Lake Trailhead

From the Taggart Lake Parking Area

The Taggart Lake trail leads to one of the most visited lakes in the park, used year-round by tourists and residents alike. It offers easy access to the base of the mountains and a variety of wildlife viewing opportunities. Trails branching off from the main loop offer options for longer hikes along the base of the mountains.

Like most of the lakes at the foot of the Tetons, Taggart and nearby Bradley lakes were formed by glaciers about 15,000 years ago when the ice piled up moraines of dirt and rocks and scoured out depressions at the mouth of each canyon. Streams that tumble out of the Tetons feed these lakes, then flow out to join Cottonwood Creek and eventually reach the Snake River.

The area accessed by the Taggart Lake Trailhead presents a fascinating opportunity to observe the relationship between the forces of geology that shaped the park and the plants and animals that now thrive here.

Most of the hiking crosses glacial moraines, where the better soil conditions support trees, shrubs, and wildflowers. The moraine you hike up and over to get to the lakes was the site of a forest fire in 1985, and the remaining dead trees, as well as the new growth, are evident along the trail.

Taggart Lake Loop

4.0 miles total, or retracing your route is 3.2 miles.

Taggart Lake Trail burn area

This is a very popular hike, both for its scenery and its convenience, but the trail can be deserted early or late in the day. The Taggart Lake Trailhead sits next to a parking lot just off the park road, and the one trail for all hikes from this point heads straight toward the mountains. The low hill directly ahead is the glacial moraine. You can see evidence of the wildfire that swept over this area years ago, and the glacial rocks and boulders are now visible without the thick forest.

At the base of the moraine the short access trail meets the loop trail and gives you the option of going left or right. Right is generally recommended for the views, but the left route is less traveled. Most visitors return on the same path they took up and don't do this loop.

The trail crosses Taggart Creek, circles past Park Service corrals and an historic old barn from the homestead era, and turns back toward the mountains. It climbs up a rocky trail along the creek until it reaches the top of the moraine, just a few hundred feet higher than the parking area. As you walk toward the mountains, the trail splits, one path going to Taggart Lake and the other to Bradley Lake. When you reach Taggart, cross the long footbridge, climb up over a low rise, and circle back down Beaver Creek to the trailhead.

Taggart Lake/Bradley Lake Loop

4.8 miles

This hike follows the same trail as the Taggart Loop until you get to the split in the trail on top of the moraine. Then you follow the sign towards Bradley Lake to the right. This trail will take you through the burned area and back out as you climb slowly up the lateral moraine that separates the two lakes.

Both moose and deer browse on the shrubs and low bushes that have established themselves here since the 1985 forest fire. One of the plants that thrives after a fire, Snowbrush, stands out with its shiny, evergreen leaves.

The trail climbs up the moraine and back down to Bradley Lake, winding through stands of pine and Douglas Fir. There are great views of the mountains all along here, and expansive views back out to the valley.

The trail circles around Bradley Lake to a marsh where moose, birds, deer, and elk are often seen. Re-trace your path to return to the trailhead or turn right when you get to the Taggart Lake fork for a longer hike.

Summer flowers

To the Lupine Meadows Parking Area

6.0 miles

If you want a moderately easy full-day hike, and you can have someone drop you off at the Taggart Lake Trailhead, you can hike all the way back to the Lupine Meadows Trailhead. About 6 miles total, this hikes offers enough variety to make it worth the effort.

Follow the trail to Bradley Lake as above and continue on around the lake to cross a footbridge. Look for birds or moose in this area. The trail continues through mixed forest as it climbs up and soon emerges into meadows. Here it cuts across the face of the hill and meets up with the Amphitheater Lake/Garnet Canyon trail. You turn right and walk downhill to the Lupine Meadows Trailhead. The trail follows a long, narrow ridge with nice views to either side.

This hike will take you through just about every kind of bird and mammal habitat, so walk quietly and pause often. This is a great walk to see wildflowers, especially early in the summer. Some of the park's more elusive flower species inhabit the bogs and shaded forest along this trail.

Short Strolls

For a great walk to stretch your legs, you can just follow the trail toward the glacial moraine, then turn either direction. This walk is flat, full of wildflowers, and has nice views. If you turn right at the junction with the loop trail, you can walk a few hundred yards to the bridge that crosses scenic little Taggart Creek.

View from the shore of Bradley Lake (right)

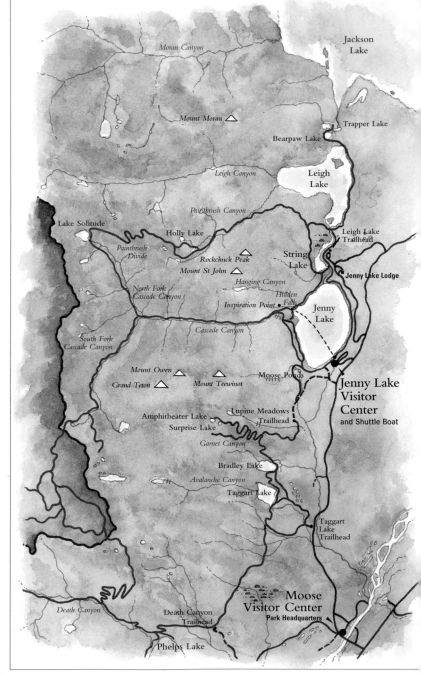

From the South Jenny Lake Area

Jenny Lake remains one of the busiest and most popular areas of the park, and it's the heart of the park trail system. You'll find up-to-date information on trail conditions, backcountry use, and camping permits at the Jenny Lake Ranger Station. The rangers here deal primarily with mountain climbers and backcountry hikers, but they also have the latest information on bears, weather, and seasonal events.

Jenny Lake is the historic center of the park as well. The first roads came here, the first trails and campgrounds were constructed nearby, and pioneer homesteaders claimed this land before the park was established. Jenny Lake inspired a long and colorful history, and many of the local buildings have stories to tell.

The boat shuttle service that carries visitors across Jenny Lake began in the 1930s as a boat rental concession. Today it offers a fast and easy way for hikers to access the Hidden Falls and Inspiration Point trails, and it gives Cascade Canyon hikers a head start on the day. The boat ride is probably most welcome to returning hikers who don't want to walk the last two miles around the lake at the end of the day. (Be sure to find out the time for the last boat crossing.)

Moose Ponds

1.5 miles round trip to Moose Ponds Overlook, 2.5 mile loop back through Lupine Meadows.

The moraine of rocks and soil damming Jenny Lake on the south side also hems in a low area between it and the base of the mountains. Small spring-fed ponds lie here and are home to moose, beaver, birds, and other wildlife. This area is especially good for wildlife first thing in the morning or late in the day.

The trail leaves the Jenny Lake area and crosses a footbridge next to the boat dock where the shuttle boats depart for Cascade Canyon. The trail follows the top of the moraine around the lake and eventually reaches the West Shore Boat Dock, Hidden Falls, and Cascade Canyon. It climbs slowly as it follows the crest of the moraine, but isn't steep.

About a half-mile from the start of the trail at the Jenny Lake footbridge, the Moose Ponds trail cuts off to the left. If you want to get a good view of where this trail leads, continue on the main trail for a few hundred yards to the Moose Ponds Overlook. Otherwise, take the Moose Ponds Trail and follow it as it circles around the ponds, over a footbridge, and winds through stands of aspen and fir trees. The trail comes out into Lupine Meadows. You can follow the gravel Lupine Trailhead road back toward Jenny Lake.

Hidden Falls

5.0 miles round trip on the Jenny Lake Trail, or 1.0 mile using the shuttle boat

Probably the most visited site in the park, the Hidden Falls area can be crowded at certain times and places. However, it's one of the places that help define the character of the park. Hiking here during quieter hours will yield more natural experiences than during midday.

If you're short on time or are unable to walk a few extra miles, you can begin at the Jenny Lake boat dock and ride the shuttle across the lake. From the West Shore Boat Dock the trail rises steeply in spots as it follows Cascade Creek, with lots of scenic places to stop and rest. After a half-mile, just before the trail crosses the creek and starts to switchback up to Inspiration Point, a short side trail leads to the falls.

This area around Hidden Falls is damp and cool, with tall Engelmann Spruce trees and shade-loving wildflowers. Pikas, small rabbit-like animals, inhabit the rocky slopes along the trail.

The alternative route to Hidden Falls begins at the South Jenny Lake Area and does not include the boat ride. This trail cuts across the base of the mountains and meets the trail to the falls at the West Shore Boat Dock.

Inspiration Point

5.8 miles round trip from the Jenny Lake Area, or 1.8 miles round trip by taking the shuttle boat

View up Cascade Canyon from Inspiration Point

Keep going for another half-mile, up into the open forest and rocky knobs that mark the beginning of Cascade Canyon, for an easy extension to the Hidden Falls hike. At Inspiration Point, the views show you how it got its name. The trail climbs sharply up after leaving the Hidden Falls area and crossing the creek, and switchbacks up the side of a rock wall to reach the viewpoint. This part of the trail often discourages hikers uncomfortable with a narrow trail and an exposed drop.

Inspiration Point presents a great destination site or a perfect stop for a rest on the way up Cascade Canyon. You'll be at about 7,000 feet elevation, and about 500 feet above Jenny Lake. You can easily see the forested moraine forming Jenny Lake and the vegetation changes that occur as the geology changes out into the center of the valley.

Hidden Falls (right)

RECEIPT

PRINTED: 07/22/06 13:25
07/22/06 13:25   POS STATION 01
INVOICE NO. 388578
CLERK: 6THNA CLERK

18397 DAY HIKES AND SHORT WALKS
1 @ 4.95   4.95 T

TOTAL ORDERED :   1
TOTAL TAKEN   :   1

SUB TOTAL   4.95
SALES TAX   0.30
PURCHASE TOTAL   5.25

LESS CASH   5.25

Upper Cascade Canyon Trail

Cascade Canyon

13 miles round trip from South Jenny Lake to the fork in the canyon, or 9 miles round trip using the boat

The Cascade Canyon Trail offers one of the gentlest slopes of any Teton trail as it follows the wide U-shaped canyon to the west of Jenny Lake.

Cascade Canyon officially starts about a half-mile up from Inspiration Point, where the steep mountain slopes squeeze closer together. From here the trail offers all kinds of terrain and habitat types, from meadow to forest to fields of boulders. It goes gently up and down, winds around, and takes you steadily into the mountains. If you lose track of how far you've walked, remember that there's a well-marked fork in the trail about 3.5 miles from Inspiration Point.

On the left as you go up, the trail reveals ever-changing views of the major Teton peaks. After a couple of miles the Grand Teton looms over the other peaks. Moose, bears, or deer may be seen on the grassy parts of the lower slopes. Moose inhabit the willows and thicker forests along Cascade Creek.

Jenny Lake Loop

7.0 miles for the full loop, or 5.0 miles taking the shuttle boat to West Shore Boat Dock first

Jenny Lake Overlook

This scenic trail around Jenny Lake was the first of the park trail system, established in 1930, and it was an immediate success. This easy, flat, and beautiful hike is a popular trail, but it's not difficult to find early or late hours when there are few other hikers.

The trail makes a full circle around Jenny Lake. Starting from the Jenny Lake Parking area, you can walk in either direction. (The hike can also be done starting from the String Lake Trailhead at the north end of the loop.) The west side, at the base of the mountains, lies mostly in shade, so on hot days it may be better to save that for the afternoon return leg. This means starting out from the Jenny Lake Parking area and heading toward the lake and the boat dock. The trail is paved for a short distance to reduce erosion and then it turns to dirt and rock.

Lodgepole Pines cover the east shore of the lake, with numerous openings and viewpoints. The scenery across the lake and up to the peaks is classic. The trail parallels the Jenny Lake one-way loop road near the middle of the lakeshore, but then it veers away from the vehicle traffic again.

At the north end, the trail reaches the String Lake Trailhead, crosses a long footbridge over the creek, and returns down the west side of Jenny Lake.

Short Strolls

Jenny Lake Trail

For a scenic stroll any time of day, walk across the footbridge at the boat dock and go left toward Lupine Meadows. There are always wildflowers and birds, and usually wildlife early in the morning. Or, you can follow the Jenny Lake Trail along the lakeshore either way to see birds, wildflowers, or an occasional moose. You can also just wander around on the paved trails and sidewalks near Jenny Lake to see wildflowers, birds, glacial rocks and boulders, and historic buildings.

String Lake

From the String Lake Parking Areas
String Lake Trailhead and Leigh Lake Trailhead

Just north of the Jenny Lake area sits String Lake, a narrow, mile-long lake connecting Jenny Lake with Leigh Lake. It can also be thought of as a wide, slow stream, since it flows steadily from one lake to the other. String Lake is a destination site as well as the starting point for a number of trails around the lakes and into the mountains. Parking areas, restrooms, a large picnic area, and two main trailheads make it a busy place in summer.

The Leigh Lake Trailhead at the String Lake Picnic Area gives access north to Leigh Lake, Trapper and Bearpaw Lakes, and into Paintbrush Canyon. The String Lake Trailhead, at the south end of the lake and close to Jenny Lake Lodge, accesses Jenny Lake and Cascade Canyon.

Both trailheads become busy at times, but early and late day hikes are usually better for avoiding crowds. Many horseback trips begin their rides into the mountains here, so you may encounter horse parties on the trails.

String Lake provides a chance to end your hike with a swim or a picnic, and it's a convenient waiting area for groups with individuals who don't hike.

To the String Lake Inlet of Jenny Lake

1 mile round trip

Jenny Lake

More of a walk than a hike, this trail can be nice any time of day. It starts at the String Lake Trailhead and crosses a long wooden footbridge. The outlet of String Lake, the stream that begins here and tumbles down to Jenny Lake, often has Dippers or Harlequin Ducks on its banks. Logs and dead trees at the outlet come from avalanches that sweep down the mountain slopes in winter.

The trail parallels the stream at a distance, winding through a Lodgepole Pine forest until it gets closer to Jenny Lake, and then the stream is visible. Once you get close to Jenny, the stream forms several deep pools before emptying into the lake. In the spring this creek can be a torrent of flood water and dangerous to approach, but in summer it's an idyllic spot to sit on a flat rock and let the music of the water drown out the world.

Leigh Lake

2 miles round trip to Leigh Lake, 4.5 miles round trip to the middle of the east shore for a good view, or another 1.7 each way to reach Bearpaw Lake

Leigh Lake

One of the real treasures of Grand Teton National Park, despite the number of visitors hiking the trail along its shoreline, Leigh Lake remains an awe-inspiring place. The trail begins at the Leigh Lake Trailhead, at the north end of the String Lake parking area, and follows the edge of String Lake for less than a mile. It divides, with the left fork crossing a long footbridge and heading up to Paintbrush Canyon and the right fork leading to Leigh Lake. Canoe parties must carry their boat from String Lake to Leigh Lake here, so don't be surprised to see a boat on the trail.

The wide, easy trail follows the gentle east shore of Leigh Lake and offers spectacular views across the water to the mountains. The water smooths out early and late in the day for photographs of the mountain reflections.

If you hike to the middle of the east lakeshore, it will be about 2 miles from the trailhead. You'll find campsites, sand beaches, and postcard scenery.

Paintbrush Divide (overleaf)

31

Marsh along west side of String Lake

String Lake Loop

3.5 miles round trip

A nice little trail loops around the lake so you don't have to backtrack over the same route. Fewer hikers use the return part of this trail. Start out by leaving the Leigh Lake Trailhead on the path to Leigh Lake, and when you get to the fork in the trail at the end of String Lake (0.8 miles), go left across the footbridge. The trail goes through Lodgepole Pines, passing several huge glacial boulders called "erratics" that look as if they were plunked down in the trees. Glaciers dropped them here long before the forest grew.

Follow this trail for a little less than a mile as it climbs a bit toward Paint-brush Canyon, until you reach another fork, well-marked, and go left back toward String Lake. The trail crosses the open slopes above String Lake and circles the south end to reach the wooden footbridge at the String Lake Trailhead. Avalanches periodically slide down this mountain during winter, sweeping away trees and vegetation. If you look at this slope from the String Lake Parking Area, you can see a crescent-shaped scar at the base of the mountain, just above the trees. This is the Teton Fault scarp, and the String Lake Loop will cross just below this geologic feature.

Paintbrush Canyon

1.6 miles to the trail junction and then another mile to get the feel of the canyon - 5 to 6 miles round trip

Holly Lake

The canyons separating the Teton peaks are incredible worlds in themselves. Paintbrush Canyon is one of the prettiest, and it's the northernmost canyon with a maintained trail. It receives less foot travel than Cascade Canyon and offers more solitude in a beautiful hike with all kinds of sights and sounds.

Take the Leigh Lake Trail from the Leigh Lake Trailhead and follow it a mile to the footbridge at the end of String Lake. Cross the bridge, go just under a mile to the junction with the Paintbrush Canyon Trail, and turn right. From here, you can walk as far as you want. Black bears often feed on wild berries, and in the early fall, elk will bugle their mating challenges.

The trail cuts around the forested northeast base of Rockchuck Peak and then turns up into the canyon. This canyon runs more north and south than the other major canyons, and it offers a different view of the mountains and different exposure to the sun and weather.

Paintbrush Canyon climbs steadily upward, with lots of rocky trail and steep sections. For a short hike you only need to go until you break out of the trees; at this point the views open up back toward Leigh Lake. The footbridge over Paintbrush Creek marks a good turn-around point, a little over three miles from the Leigh Lake Trailhead.

Known for its wildflowers, this canyon's vegetation continues to change as you hike up. For the more fit and adventurous, Holly Lake, about 6 miles from the trailhead (12 miles roundtrip), is an admirable goal.

Short Strolls

There are any number of nice strolls here on the established trails. From the String Lake Trailhead you can walk toward Jenny Lake on either the Jenny Lake Trail to the left, or cross the bridge and follow that section of trail. You can walk along the edge of String Lake on the way to Leigh Lake, and if ambitious you can go as far as the scenic wooden footbridge at the end of String Lake.

The view from Signal Mountain

From the Signal Mountain Area

Signal Mountain overlooks the west end of Jackson Lake, where the Snake River leaves the lake. Signal Mountain Lodge, on the shore of Jackson Lake, sits at the center of an area of visitor services that includes a campground, store, and boat ramp for the lake. Although this isn't a major hiking area, it offers some different kinds of walks.

This low mountain is heavily forested on the west and north sides, toward the lake and the river, but the east and southern sides are more open. A paved road leads to the top, with several viewing spots on the summit, and very few people hike the trail.

Several early pioneers built log cabins near Jackson Lake, and in the 1920s a fishing camp began operation on the lakeshore. It eventually developed into the Signal Mountain Lodge by 1940. Another major event in the area was the building of the Jackson Lake Dam during 1910-11 to raise the level of the lake and provide irrigation water for Idaho farmers. The higher water level killed about 7,000 acres of pine forest along the shores, leaving an unsightly expanse of dead trees. Crews worked from 1931 to 1937 to clean up the shores, with much of it done by the Civilian Conservation Corps.

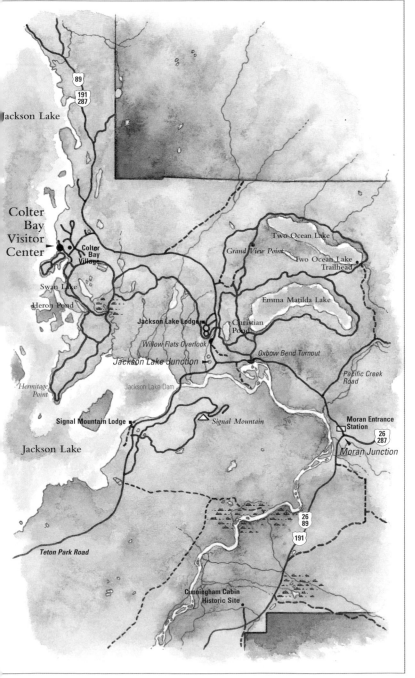

89
191
287

Jackson Lake

Colter
Bay
Visitor
Center ◄

Colter
Bay
Village

Two Ocean Lake

Grand View Point

Two Ocean Lake
Trailhead

Swan Lake

Heron Pond

Emma Matilda Lake

Jackson Lake Lodge

Christian
Pond

Willow Flats Overlook

Jackson Lake Junction ◄

Oxbow Bend Turnout

Hermitage
Point

Jackson Lake Dam

Pacific Creek
Road

Signal Mountain Lodge ◄

△ Signal Mountain

Moran Entrance
Station

26
287

Jackson Lake

Moran Junction

26
89

191

Teton Park Road

Cunningham Cabin
Historic Site

37

Teton Range and Jackson Lake at sunrise from Signal Mountain summit

The Summit of Signal Mountain

5.5 miles up to the summit and back down, or 2.8 miles one-way

Besides the aerial ski tram on the park's southern border, Signal Mountain provides the only place you can hike downhill all the way. Situated in the heart of the park, it offers great views of the entire Teton Range across Jackson Lake, the Snake River channels, and the Jackson Hole valley.

There are several options for hiking this trail. You can walk from the base to the top, or from the top down. You can also hike up and then back down. The trail begins at the Signal Mountain area, and it's best to park near the lodge and walk back out to the main road. Turn right, and about two hundred yards down, across the road, there's a small sign and a trail. You can also reach the trail by driving south to the Signal Mountain Road, going a mile to a small pond and turnout on the right, and parking there. The trail can be picked up along the right side of the pond. Soon after this there is a fork in the trail. This is actually a detour, or loop, and you can go either way. To the right is recommended, going up past the ponds and coming back down the ridge. If you wish, at the far end of this loop you could return on the other leg, without going on to the summit.

The trail climbs steadily but not overly so and eventually reaches Jackson Point Overlook, where you can be met by car. This entire hike has potential for wildlife, wildflowers, songbirds, and views.

At one time the trail continued around the east side of Signal Mountain and crossed the Snake River on a bridge near the Oxbow Bend area, and maps still show it, but that crossing is gone.

Short Strolls

Signal Mountain is a great place for strolling. From the main parking area you can find your way to the lakeshore and walk along it. As the summer progresses, the lake level drops and more beach is exposed. You can also walk on the paved road toward the boat ramp, then walk to the left on the gravel beach or on a footpath through the trees. Another nice place to walk is near the pond one mile in on the Signal Mountain Road. The summit also has some scenic short trails and paths to its overlooks.

Calf moose (right)

View from Jackson Lake Lodge

From the Jackson Lake Lodge Area

Jackson Lake Lodge opened in 1922, with cabins, tents, and guided trips. It was the first lodge in the valley with hot and cold running water, and toilets. In 1930 the Snake River Land Company purchased it and eventually replaced it with the present lodge buildings in the 1950s. The lodge sits on a high bench overlooking the broad willow flats that border Jackson Lake.

This area of the park teems with wildlife, and many of the hikes on the area trails wind through prime habitat. Most wildlife species prefer to inhabit places that have a mix of vegetation, terrain, and water, and these trails take advantage of the local conditions.

To the east lie two small glacial lakes, Emma Matilda and Two Ocean, and then the vast Teton Wilderness. Within just a few miles of the lodge you'll find marshes, a river, several lakes, meadows, foothills, and forest. The trails in this area provide great bird-watching and wildflower shows.

Christian Pond Loop

3.7 miles

The pond in this beautiful little area of the park was named for Charlie Christian, who worked on the Jackson Lake Dam construction and then took up a 160-acre homestead here in 1916. He picked an area that may not have been good ranching, but it turned out to be great for wildlife. This is one of the more regular spots in the park to see moose.

The trail begins at a small parking area along the park road, across from the entrance road to Jackson Lake Lodge. You can also follow the horse trail that leaves the lodge area horse corral and goes under the highway bridge. The trails meet and lead to the right, across Christian Creek, and up to a low overlook. This is a good place to observe moose or Trumpeter Swans from a distance.

The trail continues on around the pond, and you keep bearing left until you return to the parking area by the highway. This is mostly open meadows, willow thickets, and sagebrush. An ideal short hike for early morning or late afternoon bird-watching, the variety of habitats makes it good for finding a wide range of wildflowers.

Emma Matilda

4.6 miles round trip to view of the lake

Emma Matilda Lake Trail

Just over the hill beyond Christian Pond is Emma Matilda Lake, named for the wife of William Owen, who made the first documented ascent of the Grand Teton. Emma Matilda Lake was surveyed for a dam in the 1920s, but the plan was blocked by the Park Service.

The trail starts out the same as if hiking around Christian Pond, but after leaving the Christian Pond Overlook you turn right at the next intersection, toward the Oxbow Bend. This trail loops around through sagebrush meadows on the hills above the Oxbow and then turns left toward Emma Matilda. You can either take the Lookout Rock cutoff or stay on the Oxbow Bend Trail to end up in the same place at the lake.

This trail offers wonderful views of the mountains, Jackson Lake, the Oxbow Bend of the Snake River, and Emma Matilda Lake. You can extend this hike into an 11-mile hike by turning right when you get to Emma Matilda and circling the lake to meet the north loop of the Christian Pond Trail.

Willow Flats

Willow Flats

4.8 miles round trip to the bridge and back

For something completely different, you might want to try this hike, especially if you like birds, wildflowers, and a flat trail. The path starts at the Willow Flats Overlook, or you can catch it behind the Jackson Lake Lodge. It follows an old dirt road connected to Colter Bay Village and is used infrequently by lodge vehicles, so it's not exactly a wilderness hike. It cuts through classic willow and wetlands habitat that can be full of wildlife. Sandhill Cranes and other wading birds, moose, coyotes, and all sorts of songbirds live here. Willows are the primary food of moose in the winter.

This trail is wide open to the sky, so it's best to hike it early or late in the day. After about 2.5 miles the trail reaches a very obvious bridge over Pilgrim Creek. This marks a good turning point for an easy hike. The bridge remains from the days when this path was the road to Yellowstone.

If you want to continue on, you cross the bridge and walk until you hit an intersection. You can go either direction. If you stay right on the dirt road, follow it until you intersect with the Third Creek Trail coming from the left. Take it for half a mile, and then at the next intersection turn left again, back toward Willow Flats. You'll go through the picnic area on Second Creek, and reconnect with the main dirt road. This loop will add just under 4 miles.

Short Strolls

There are any number of nice strolls to take around here. The short walk out to the Christian Pond Overlook is always interesting, as are the first few hundred yards of the Willow Flats Trail. The extensive parking areas of Jackson Lake Lodge are actually lined with native trees and wildflowers and offer decent bird watching early in the morning.

Trumpter Swan (right), Elk on Willow Flats (overleaf)

From the Two Ocean Lake Trailhead

As a nice diversion from the dramatic mountain trails in the Tetons, this part of the park offers a bit of solitude and excellent wildlife and wildflower experiences. Two Ocean Lake and nearby Emma Matilda are two of the oldest lakes in the park, formed about 20,000-25,000 years ago by glaciers. They are hemmed in by the moraines of soil and rock deposited by the glaciers as they melted.

Pacific Creek Road, between the Moran Junction and Jackson Lake Junction, leads to the marked turn-off to Two Ocean Lake. There's a small picnic area and toilet facility at the lake, but for the most part this area feels fairly undeveloped. Canoeists and fishermen occasionally use the lake.

Since Two Ocean Lake is just a mile from the rugged and remote country of the Teton Wilderness, it presents one of the best chances to look for the tracks of wolves, grizzly bears, or mountain lions. These animals are generally reclusive and try to avoid people, but they may pass by the lake during the night.

Two Ocean Lake is considered a place for solitude, and most of its visitors come here to listen to wild songbirds, hear elk bugle in the fall, or find a sunny meadow for a quiet picnic. Emma Matilda gets even less visitation, and is reached by a trail from the Two Ocean Lake Trailhead.

Two Ocean Lake

Two Ocean Lake Loop

6.4 miles round trip

Two Ocean Lake is the geologic twin to Emma Matilda Lake, which lies just over a ridge to the south. Its name comes from the nearby Two Ocean Plateau, where streams may go west toward the Pacific or east toward the Atlantic.

Two Ocean Lake is quiet and tree-lined with beautiful scenery and lots of wildlife. Since it's far from the excitement of the Tetons, it gets very little visitor use.

You'll find the Two Ocean Lake Trailhead at the end of a dirt road that forks off the Pacific Creek Road, just north of the Moran Entrance Station. In spring or during rainstorms, this road can be muddy. The trailhead and pic-nic site are at the east end of the lake.

The well-marked trail circles the lake. The route to the right is generally preferred since it offers the best mountain views as you walk. It cuts through meadows, marshes, and mixed stands of trees all the way to the other end of the lake, 3 miles away. Bears inhabit this area, so be familiar with the infor-mation in the park handouts for hiking in bear country. Encounters are rare, but you may see tracks or other sign.

At the far end of the lake the trail intersects with the trail to Grand View Point. Keep going left to follow the trail back to the trailhead where you started. The total loop is a little over 6 miles of easy walking.

Two Ocean Loop plus Grand View Point

9 miles round trip

Jackson Lake from Grand View Point

For a slightly longer and more rigorous hike, you can add on the trail up to Grand View Point and back, at the far end of Two Ocean Lake. This will add about 2.6 miles. From the lake loop, the trail takes off to the right and climbs 700 feet through the forest to a high and spectacular viewpoint.

The trail switchbacks up to the summit, and it can be difficult after already hiking to the end of Two Ocean Lake. Wildflowers are usually abundant along the trail, and since the area isn't visited much there are often deer and elk. This trail can have snow or mud early in the season. The road into Two Ocean Lake remains closed until the snow has melted sufficiently to drive, but the trails may still have patches.

If the Two Ocean Lake Road is closed, you can often reach Grand View Point from the west. There's a dirt road to the right off the highway, just a mile north of the Jackson Lake Lodge. It takes you to the Grand View Point Trailhead, where it's a little over a mile hike to the viewpoint. This access road is rocky and isn't recommended for low clearance vehicles.

A nice short hike leaves the Two Ocean Trailhead and goes up to the ridge between Two Ocean Lake and Emma Matilda Lake. This is about a mile each way.

Short Strolls

Two Ocean Lake from Grand View Point

From the Two Ocean Lake Trailhead, you can walk to the north (right) through beautiful little stands of trees and open meadows. You can also walk back along the Two Ocean Road and look for wildlife. On the other side, at the Grand View Point Trailhead, you can walk along the dirt road at the base of the hills. This is an excellent wildflower area.

View of Mount Moran from Colter Bay

From the Colter Bay Area and Hermitage Point Trailhead

Colter Bay, the northernmost large development in the park, includes all the amenities of dining, lodging, and marina service. Some of its older cabins arrived in the 1950s, when the original Jackson Lake Lodge nearby was removed to make way for the present building. Colter Bay sits in a unique spot in the park, on the forested east shore of Jackson Lake, with great views across the water.

From here the Teton Mountains make spectacular scenery but are not accessible by trail. The surrounding landscape offers interesting and easily explored country with good access to the shoreline of the lake and its ever-changing moods. Miles of trails explore the convoluted lakeshore with its bays, points, ponds, and meadows. Other trails connect with those coming from Jackson Lake Lodge.

This is a good area for hikers and non-hikers to share the day. While some people hike to viewpoints along the lake, the rest of the party can visit the fascinating Colter Bay Indian Arts museum, stroll the shoreline, or take to the water in a rental canoe.

The trails here are all more or less flat, with moderate up-and-down sections, and there are lots of short-trip destinations with abundant wildlife, wildflowers, and great scenery.

49

The Lakeshore Trail

2.0 miles round trip

Mount Moran at sunset from Lake Shore Trail

This short walk is a nice introduction to the kind of landscape surrounding the Colter Bay area. It's perfect for a very early morning walk to watch the sunrise hit the Tetons, or for having a sunset picnic on the lakeshore.

Paved pathways near the boat dock and visitor center lead to the north (right) and a paved trail that then becomes a path through the trees. After reaching the end of a short peninsula, it crosses a dike and goes to a forested island. The trail circles the perimeter of this island and returns to re-cross the dike.

On the far western end of the island, panoramic views stretch across Jackson Lake to the Tetons. The lake can be rough at times, especially in the afternoons, but it often calms down late in the day. Early in the morning it can be like glass. This trail is short enough that you can quickly reach the end of the island during the calm hours, for photographs or just for the view.

The water level of Jackson Lake was raised almost 40 feet by the dam built in 1910. This extra water is drained off during the summer months to irrigate farms in neighboring Idaho, so the lake level may drop, exposing more of the rocky shoreline. Jackson Lake is open for fishing, but check at the visitor center for seasons and license information.

Heron Pond and Swan Lake

3.0 miles round trip

Just south of Colter Bay Village lies a series of ponds, marshes, meadows, and open forests that form a large area of prime wildlife habitat.

From the end of the parking lot near the boat dock and marina, take the marked trail toward Hermitage Point. It starts as a dirt road and then turns into a trail. The trail follows near the shore of the lake for just under a half-mile and then intersects the Swan Lake Trail. Turn right, toward the mountains and the lake. This will take you to Heron Pond, with a detour up to the Jackson Lake Overlook if you want. Both routes arrive at Heron Pond, where there are usually various kinds of waterfowl, beavers, and sometimes a moose.

At the end of the pond go left at the intersection to Swan Lake. There may actually be Trumpeter Swans on Swan Lake on occasion. The total hike on this path is about 3 miles of easy walking, with a few ups and downs.

Hermitage Point

Hermitage Point

9.2 miles round trip

From the air, Colter Bay and the east shore of Jackson Lake look like the edge of a partially completed jigsaw puzzle. Contoured bays, barely connected islands, and narrow peninsulas form the shoreline. At the end, Hermitage Point juts way out into the lake, almost due west of the Jackson Lake Dam.

From the Hermitage Point Trailhead, described above, follow the trail to the end of Heron Pond and then turn right, along the lakeshore. After a mile there's a shortcut to the left, but stay right. This eventually takes you out of the forest and into sagebrush, wide views, and to the end of the point of land. It's about 4.5 miles from your car to this farthest point.

You continue on the trail as it rounds the end of the point and heads back along the east side. You pass a campground, and about two miles from the point there's a shortcut trail to the left. Skip that one, but take the next left about three-quarters of a mile later. This will return you to the south end of Heron Pond, where you can retrace your path to the parking area or go right and see Swan Lake. This route is described in the Swan Lake section.

Short Strolls

From the Colter Bay Area, there are some nice strolls along the Lake Shore Trail as far as the dike, down the Hermitage Point Trail a short distance for a view. If you prefer to stay on pavement, you can walk all the way up to the Colter Bay horse corral.

Heron Pond (overleaf)

Other Short Strolls in the Park

Mormon Row

Mormon Row barn

This historic old lane crosses the Antelope Flats Road at the north end of Blacktail Butte. There are several small parking areas near the abandoned ranch buildings where the roads cross. This is also good bison and pronghorn country, and early in the summer there are large wildflower blooms.

Blacktail Butte

Rainbow at Blacktail Butte

There's a small parking area at the north end of Blacktail Butte, and an unimproved trail that follows the base of the hill back to the south. You'll pass a "borrow pit" on the right, where rock was taken to build the highway in the 1950s, on the way to a tree-lined meadow where an old homestead was once located.

Menor's Ferry

Menor's Ferry General Store

Bill and Holiday Menor were two old bachelors who homesteaded here and built a ferry across the Snake River. You can park at the Chapel of the Transfiguration and wander around the old buildings next to the river. There are a number of historic cabins and displays scattered around the area.

Jackson Lake Dam

Two bull moose on Jackson Lake Dam

Paved parking lots sit on both sides of the dam. On the north side there's a large site, toilets, and access to the river. Walk along the gravel river bank and you may see Ospreys, Bald Eagles, Pelicans, or an occasional river otter. On the south side you're high above the river. You can walk down to it on a wide path at the end of the parking area, or cross the highway and walk on a footpath toward the mountains.

Spalding Bay Road

Black bear cubs

Just north of the North Jenny Lake Junction a gravel access road leads to Spalding Bay on Jackson Lake. This is a rough road and not recommended for travel. There's a large vehicle turnaround area just off the pavement where you can park and walk down the gravel road. Wildflowers, picturesque old trees, and birds are found here.

River Road (RKO)

Mountain Bluebird

Just south of the Signal Mountain Road, a rough gravel road heads toward the Snake River and eventually comes out near Cottonwood Creek. Only 4-wheel drive vehicles survive this road, but the first half-mile or so is a good place to walk and look for wildflowers, birds, and elk or pronghorn.

©2005 Grand Teton Natural History Association
Grand Teton National Park
P.O. Box 170, Moose WY 83012
www.grandtetonpark.org

Design and Production by
Jeff Pollard Design & Associates

Maps by
Mike Reagan

Project Coordinated by
Jan Lynch, Executive Director,
Grand Teton Natural History Association

Printed by
Paragon Press

ISBN 0-931895-62-6